To

....

From

....

Date

....

$\mathcal{D}$o not be afraid, for behold,
I bring you good tidings of great joy
which will be to all people.
For there is born to you this day
in the city of David a Savior,
who is Christ the Lord.

LUKE 2:10-11 NKJV

Jesus Is the Reason for the Season

CELEBRATE THE TRUE MEANING OF CHRISTMAS

Pi Pocket
INSPIRATIONS

summerside
PRESS

Summerside Press™
Minneapolis, MN 55337
www.summersidepress.com

Jesus Is the Reason for the Season

ISBN 978-1-60936-247-8

Compilation by Rebecca Currington in association with Snapdragon
Group℠, Tulsa, OK.

Cover and interior design by Jeff Jansen, Aesthetic Soup
Layout and typesetting by Stephanie D. Walker—water2winedesign.com

*Summerside Press™ is an inspirational publisher offering fresh, irresistible books
to uplift the heart and engage the mind.*

Printed in the USA.

Introduction

Christmas. Stop for a moment and think about all that one special word means. Family, friends, parties, music, food, gifts, memories, a tree, and so much more. It's not just a special day; it's a much-anticipated time of year. No wonder the "reason for the season" is sometimes overlooked, buried beneath all our Christmas traditions and trappings.

First and foremost, Christmas is about Jesus. It's a celebration of His birth, and His birthday is like no other. It's the day when God clothed His Son in an earthly body and gave Him to all mankind. It is the day we received a gift of unspeakable value. Once here, Jesus became the embodiment of His Father's love and the means of our reconciliation to Him.

Jesus Is the Reason for the Season is meant to be a reminder of God's great love for us and His plan to bring us into His family. We pray as you read through these pages, you will feel hope rising for a future as bright as the stars of heaven. Read slowly and take it all in. It's the greatest story ever told, inspired by the greatest love ever given. We pray it will bring you the greatest joy you've ever experienced in this wonderful season.

*T*he coming of Christ by way of a Bethlehem
manger seems strange and stunning. But when
we take him out of the manger and invite
him into our hearts, then the meaning unfolds
and the strangeness vanishes.

NEIL C. STRAIT

What You May Not Know About Christmas

You might be surprised to learn that in the early years of Christianity, Easter was the primary holiday. It wasn't until the fourth century that church officials created a holiday to celebrate the birth of Christ. Puritans were quick to point out that the Bible does not mention *when* Jesus was born. Logically, it would have been in the spring since shepherds were herding their sheep. But Pope Julius I chose December 25 instead. His reasoning is unclear, but he may have reasoned that choosing the same time as the winter solstice festivals would give the holiday a popular following. And it worked, though not without some egregious consequences.

The holiday, referred to as the Feast of the Nativity, collided with the pagan Saturnalia festival. By the Middle Ages, celebrants first attended church and then participated in a drunken, carnival-like street party reminiscent of today's Mardi Gras. As part of the celebration, a beggar would be chosen and crowned the "lord of misrule," while the other revelers served as his subjects. The crowds, primarily made up of the poor, would go to the homes of the wealthy and demand their best food and drink. If the homeowners refused, the crowd would harass them with mischief.

By the 17th century, these practices were widely criticized by the Puritans. When Oliver Cromwell and the Puritans took over England in 1645, Christmas was officially cancelled. Of course, as soon as Charles II was restored to the throne, it was reinstated by popular demand.

When the Pilgrims came to America, they were even more conservative than their Puritan brothers and sisters. Christmas was not celebrated in the New World. In fact from 1659-1681, it was outlawed in Boston. Offenders were fined five shillings. Other parts of the colonies enjoyed a quieter, more civilized holiday until after the American Revolution, at which point, all English customs fell out of favor. Christmas wasn't declared a federal holiday until June 26, 1870.

Christmas Cheese Tree

1 (8 ounce) package extra sharp cheddar
    cheese, shredded
1 (8-ounce) package medium cheddar
    cheese, shredded.
¼ cup grated onion
½ cup mayonnaise
½ teaspoon red pepper
1 cup chopped fresh parsley
Fresh cranberries

Combine extra sharp cheddar cheese and
medium cheddar cheese, onion, mayonnaise,
and red pepper. Mix well and shape into a cone.
Press the chopped parsley onto the cheese cone,
covering all surfaces. Place cranberries on the
tree as ornaments. Serve with crackers. Yield: 1
cheese tree

Christmas Eve Prayer

FRANK BORMAN
APOLLO 8 SPACE MISSION, 1968

Give us, O God, the vision which can see Your love in the world in spite of human failure.

Give us the faith to trust Your goodness in spite of our ignorance and weakness.

Give us the knowledge that we may continue to pray with understanding hearts.

And show us what each one of us can do to set forward the coming of the day of universal peace.

Jesus Is the Reason
for the Season

Thou Christmas Babe

When mother love makes all things bright,
When joy comes with the morning light,
When children gather round their tree,
Thou, Christmas Babe, we sing of thee!

TUDOR JENKS

The Hallelujah Chorus from Messiah

Hallelujah! Hallelujah! Hallelujah! Hallelujah!
Hallelujah!
For the Lord God Omnipotent reigneth.
Hallelujah! Hallelujah! Hallelujah! Hallelujah!
For the Lord God omnipotent reigneth.
Hallelujah! Hallelujah! Hallelujah! Hallelujah!
Hallelujah! Hallelujah! Hallelujah!
The kingdom of this world
Is become the kingdom of our Lord,
And of His Christ, and of His Christ;
And He shall reign for ever and ever,
For ever and ever, forever and ever,
King of kings, and Lord of lords,
King of kings, and Lord of lords,
And Lord of lords,
And He shall reign,
And He shall reign forever and ever,
King of kings, forever and ever,
And Lord of lords,
Hallelujah! Hallelujah!
And He shall reign forever and ever,

King of kings! and Lord of lords!
And He shall reign forever and ever,
King of kings! and Lord of lords!
Hallelujah! Hallelujah! Hallelujah! Hallelujah!
Hallelujah!

No Christmas season is complete without attending a performance of George Frideric Handel's *Messiah*. And though many have become familiar with large portions of the oratorio, its majestic *Hallelujah Chorus* has gained great popularity.

This beautiful composition was not typical for Handel, a vigorous champion of Italian opera. *Messiah* is different from any of Handel's earlier works. Unlike an opera, it tells no story. Instead it can be described as a commentary of Christ's nativity, passion, resurrection, and ascension, beginning with God's promises as spoken by the prophets and ending with Christ's glorification in heaven. In contrast to Handel's earlier oratorios, the singers in *Messiah* do not assume dramatic roles, there is not a single, dominant narrative voice, and very little use of direct speech.

The three-part structure of *Messiah* is

equivalent to Handel's three-act operas, though the parts are subdivided into scenes. It is compiled almost exclusively from the King James Version of the Bible and the Book of Common Prayer.

Handel received the text for *Messiah* from Charles Jennens, a country squire with musical and literary talents, in July 1741. The text was accompanied by a letter from Jennens to Handel encouraging him to "lay out his whole genius and skill upon it as the subject excels every other subject."

Having received the text some time after July 10, Handel's notes state that he began work about six weeks later on August 22. The startling fact is that he finished on September 14. He had completed the composition of this masterpiece in 24 days!

Handel signed his work with three letters "SDG" (Soli Deo Gloria) which means "to the only God glory." Many feel that Handel wrote *Messiah* in a frenzy of divine inspiration, though most of his forty operas were written just as quickly.

A few years before composing *Messiah*, Handel suffered a stroke that left his right arm paralyzed and his vision blurred. He was unable to conduct or perform on the keyboard or piano.

In addition, his on-again-off-again relationship with King George left him in financial jeopardy. This was coupled with the fact that Handel was not a wise businessman and had lost a fortune in the opera business. By the time, he received the text from Jennens, he was depressed and deeply in debt. When Handel received the text from Jennens, it must have seemed to him that God had given him a gift, a chance to redeem himself.

And indeed, King George did decide to attend a performance of the work. It is said that when the *Hallelujah Chorus* began to play, the King was so moved that he could not stay in his seat. When he abruptly stood to his feet, many took his action to indicate that he recognized Christ as the King of Kings. Since it was considered protocol for everyone to stand when the king was standing, the entire audience followed his lead. Today, the tradition endures, with audiences standing in reverence while the Hallelujah Chorus is performed.

Handel's *Messiah* received only limited success before his death in 1759. The greatest number of performances were given on behalf of London's Foundling Hospital. After his death however, his score was drastically reorchestrated to suit contemporary tastes. Large scale performances with hundreds of singers and instruments prevailed and *Messiah* was altered to comply. This trend continued through into the 20th century.

Finally, there was a call for performances more faithful to Handel's original concept. Some returned to Handel's original notes, hoping to find a purer version. These days, many performances strive for authenticity, but it is generally agreed that there can never be a definitive performance of *Messiah*. The surviving manuscripts are radically different for many of the numbers, both vocal and instrumental.

Regardless of its evolution since Handel first put his pen to paper, *Messiah* has left an impressive mark on the hearts and minds of those who hear his stirring masterpiece and find themselves caught up in worship.

DID YOU KNOW?

*E*ach year, 30-35 million real Christmas trees are sold in the United States alone. There are 21,000 Christmas tree growers in the United States, and trees usually grow for about 15 years before they are sold.

*T*he way to Christmas lies through an ancient gate. It is a little gate, child-high, child-wide, and there is a password:
"Peace on earth to men of good will."
May you, this Christmas, become as a little child again and enter into His kingdom.

ANGELO PATRI

Thanks be to God for his unspeakable Gift—
Indescribable
Inestimable
Incomparable
Inexpressible
Precious beyond words.

LOIS LEBAR

The Gift of the Magi

BY O. HENRY

One dollar and eighty-seven cents. That was all. And sixty cents of it was in pennies. Pennies saved one and two at a time by bulldozing the grocer and the vegetable man and the butcher until one's cheeks burned with the silent imputation of parsimony that such close dealing implied. Three times Della counted it. One dollar and eighty-seven cents. And the next day would be Christmas.

There was clearly nothing to do but flop down on the shabby little couch and howl. So Della did it. Which instigates the moral reflection that life is made up of sobs, sniffles, and smiles, with sniffles predominating.

While the mistress of the home is gradually subsiding from the first stage to the second, take a look at the home. A furnished flat at $8 per week. It did not exactly fit beggar description, but it certainly had that word on the lookout for the mendicancy squad.

In the vestibule below was a letter-box into which no letter would go, and an electric button from which no mortal finger could coax a ring. Also appertaining thereunto was a card bearing the name "Mr. James Dillingham Young."

The "Dillingham" had been flung to the breeze during a former period of prosperity when its possessor was being paid $30 per week. Now, when the income was shrunk to $20, the letters of "Dillingham" look blurred, as though they were thinking seriously of contracting to a modest and unassuming D. But whenever Mr. James Dillingham Young came home and reached his flat above he was called "Jim" and greatly hugged by Mrs. James Dillingham Young, already introduced to you as Della. Which is all very good.

Della finished her cry and attended to her cheeks with the powder rag. She stood by the window and looked out dully at a gray cat walking a gray fence in a gray backyard. Tomorrow would be Christmas Day, and she had only $1.87 with which to buy Jim a present. She had been saving every penny she could for months, with this result. Twenty dollars a week doesn't go far. Expenses had been greater than she had calculated. They always are. Only $1.87 to buy a present for Jim. Her Jim. Many a happy hour she had spent planning for something nice for him. Something fine and rare and sterling— something just a little bit near to being worthy of the honor of being owned by Jim.

There was a pier-glass between the windows

of the room. Perhaps you have seen a pier-glass in an $8 flat. A very thin and very agile person may, by observing his reflection in a rapid sequence of longitudinal strips, obtain a fairly accurate conception of his looks. Della, being slender, had mastered the art.

Suddenly she whirled from the window and stood before the glass. Her eyes were shining brilliantly, but her face had lost its color within twenty seconds. Rapidly she pulled down her hair and let it fall to its full length.

Now, there were two possessions of the James Dillingham Youngs in which they both took a mighty pride. One was Jim's gold watch that had been his father's and his grandfather's. The other was Della's hair. Had the Queen of Sheba lived in the flat across the airshaft, Della would have let her hair hang out the window some day to dry just to depreciate Her Majesty's jewels and gifts. Had King Solomon been the janitor, with all his treasures piled up in the basement, Jim would have pulled out his watch every time he passed, just to see him pluck at his beard from envy.

So now Della's beautiful hair fell about her rippling and shining like a cascade of brown waters. It reached below her knee and made itself almost a garment for her. And then she did it up again nervously and quickly. Once she faltered for a minute and stood still while a tear or two splashed on the worn red carpet.

On went her old brown jacket; on went her old brown hat. With a whirl of skirts and with the brilliant sparkle still in her eyes, she fluttered out the door and down the stairs to the street.

Where she stopped the sign read: "Mme. Sofronie. Hair Goods of All Kinds." One flight up Della ran, and collected herself, panting. Madame, large, too white, chilly, hardly looked the "Sofronie."

"Will you buy my hair?" asked Della.

"I buy hair," said Madame. "Take yer hat off and let's have a sight at the looks of it."

Down rippled the brown cascade.

"Twenty dollars," said Madame, lifting the mass with a practiced hand.

"Give it to me quick," said Della.

Oh, and the next two hours tripped by on rosy wings. Forget the hashed metaphor. She was ransacking the stores for Jim's present.

She found it at last. It surely had been made for Jim and no one else. There was no other like it in any of the stores, and she had turned all of them inside out. It was a platinum fob chain simple and chaste in design, properly proclaiming its value by substance alone and not by meretricious ornamentation—as all good things should do. It was even worthy of The Watch. As soon as she saw it she knew that it must be Jim's. It was like him. Quietness and value—the description applied to both. Twenty-one dollars they took from her for it, and she hurried home with the 87 cents. With that chain on his watch Jim might be properly anxious about the time in any company. Grand as the watch was, he sometimes looked at it on the sly on account of the old leather strap that he used in place of a chain.

When Della reached home her intoxication gave way a little to prudence and reason. She got out her curling irons and lighted the gas and went to work repairing the ravages made by generosity added to love. Which is always a tremendous task, dear friends—a mammoth task.

Within forty minutes her head was covered with tiny, close-lying curls that made her look wonderfully like a truant school-boy. She looked at her reflection in the mirror long, carefully, and critically.

"If Jim doesn't kill me," she said to herself, "before he takes a second look at me, he'll say I look like a Coney Island chorus girl. But what could I do—oh! What could I do with a dollar and eighty-seven cents?"

At 7 o'clock the coffee was made and the frying-pan was on the back of the stove hot and ready to cook the chops.

Jim was never late. Della doubled the fob chain in her hand and sat on the corner of the table near the door that he always entered. Then she heard his step on the stairway down on the first flight, and she turned white for just a moment. She had a habit of saying little silent prayers about the simplest everyday things, and now she whispered: "Please God, make him think I am still pretty."

The door opened and Jim stepped in and closed it. He looked thin and very serious. Poor fellow, he was only twenty-two—and to be burdened with a family! He needed a new overcoat and he was without gloves.

Jim stopped inside the door, as immovable as a setter at the scent of quail. His eyes were fixed upon Della, and there was an expression in them that she could not read, and it terrified her. It was not anger, nor surprise, nor disapproval, nor horror, nor any of the sentiments that she had been prepared for. He simply stared at her fixedly with that peculiar expression on his face.

Della wriggled off the table and went for him.

"Jim, darling," she cried, "don't look at me

that way. I had my hair cut off and sold it because I couldn't have lived through Christmas without giving you a present. It'll grow out again—you won't mind, will you? I just had to do it. My hair grows awfully fast. Say 'Merry Christmas!' Jim, and let's be happy. You don't know what a nice—what a beautiful, nice gift I've got for you."

"You've cut off your hair?" asked Jim, laboriously, as if he had not arrived at that patent fact yet even after the hardest mental labor.

"Cut if off and sold it," said Della. "Don't you like me just as well, anyhow? I'm me without my hair, ain't I?"

Jim looked about the room curiously.

"You say your hair is gone?" he said, with an air almost of idiocy.

"You needn't look for it," said Della. "It's sold, I tell you—sold and gone, too. It's Christmas Eve, boy. Be good to me, for it went for you. Maybe the hairs of my head were numbered," she went on with a sudden serious sweetness, "but nobody could ever count my love for you. Shall I put the chops on, Jim?"

Out of his trance Jim seemed quickly to wake. He enfolded his Della. For ten seconds let us regard with discreet scrutiny some inconsequential object in the other direction.

Eight dollars a week or a million a year—what is the difference? A mathematician or a wit would give you the wrong answer. The magi brought valuable gifts, but that was not among them. This dark assertion will be illuminated later on.

Jim drew a package from his overcoat pocket and threw it upon the table.

"Don't make any mistake, Dell," he said, "about me. I don't think there's anything in the way of a haircut or a shave that could make me like my girl any less. But if you'll unwrap that package, you may see why you had me going a while at first."

White fingers and nimble tore at the string and paper. And then an ecstatic scream of joy; and then, alas! A quick feminine change to hysterical tears and wails, necessitating the immediate employment of all the comforting powers of the lord of the flat.

For there lay The Combs—the set of combs, side and back, that Della had worshipped for long in a Broadway window. Beautiful combs, pure tortoise shell, with jeweled rims—just the shade to wear in the beautiful vanished hair. They were expensive combs, she knew, and her heart had simply craved and yearned over them without the least hope of possession. And now, they were hers, but the tresses that should have adorned the coveted adornments were gone.

But she hugged them to her bosom, and at length she was able to look up with dim eyes and a smile and say: "My hair grows so fast, Jim!"

And then Della leaped up like a little singed cat and cried, "Oh, oh!"

Jim had not yet seen his beautiful present. She held it out to him eagerly upon her open palm. The dull precious metal seemed to flash with a reflection of her bright and ardent spirit.

"Isn't it a dandy, Jim? I hunted all over town to find it. You'll have to look at the time a hundred times a day now. Give me your watch. I want to see how it looks on it."

Instead of obeying, Jim tumbled down on the couch and put his hands under the back of his head and smiled.

"Dell," said he, "let's put our Christmas presents away and keep 'em a while. They're too nice to use just at present. I sold the watch to get the money to buy your combs. And now supposed you put the chops on."

The magi, as you know, were wise men—wonderfully wise men—who brought gifts to the Babe in the manger. They invented the art of giving Christmas presents. Being wise, their gifts were no doubt wise ones, possibly bearing the privilege of exchange in case of duplication. And here I have lamely related to you the uneventful chronicle of two foolish children in a flat who most unwisely sacrificed for each other the greatest treasures of their house. But in a last word to the wise of these days let it be said that of all who give gifts these two were the wisest. Of all who give and receive gifts, such as they are the wisest. Everywhere they are wisest. They are the magi.

*The most vivid memories of Christmases past
are usually not of gifts given or received,
but of the spirit of love,
the special warmth of Christmas worship,
the cherished little habits of the home,
the results of others acting
in the spirit of Christ.*

Lois Rand

The Birth of Jesus Foretold

LUKE 1:26–38 NIV

God sent the angel Gabriel to Nazareth, a town in Galilee, to a virgin pledged to be married to a man named Joseph, a descendant of David. The virgin's name was Mary. The angel went to her and said, "Greetings, you who are highly favored! The Lord is with you."

Mary was greatly troubled at his words and wondered what kind of greeting this might be. But the angel said to her, "Do not be afraid, Mary; you have found favor with God. You will be with child and give birth to a son, and you are to give him the name Jesus. He will be great and will be called the Son of the Most High. The Lord God will give him the throne of his father David, and he will reign over the house of Jacob forever; his kingdom will never end."

"How will this be," Mary asked the angel, "since I am a virgin?"

The angel answered, "The Holy Spirit will come upon you, and the power of the Most High will overshadow you. So the holy one to be born will be called the Son of God. Even Elizabeth your relative is going to have a child in her old age, and she who was said to be barren is in her sixth month. For nothing is impossible with God."

"I am the Lord's servant," Mary answered. "May it be to me as you have said," Then the angel left her.

Mary Visits Elizabeth

LUKE 1:39-56 NIV

At that time Mary got ready and hurried to a town in the hill country of Judea, where she entered Zechariah's home and greeted Elizabeth. When Elizabeth heard Mary's greeting, the baby leaped in her womb, and Elizabeth was filled with the Holy Spirit. In a loud voice she exclaimed: "Blessed are you among women, and blessed is the child you will bear. But why am I so favored that the mother of my Lord should come to me? As soon as the sound of your greeting reached my ears, the baby in my womb leaped for joy. Blessed is she who has believed that what the Lord has said to her will be accomplished!"

Mary's Song

And Mary said:
"My soul glorifies the Lord
　　and my spirit rejoices in God
　　　　my Savior,
for he has been mindful
　　of the humble state of his servant.
From now on all generations
　　　　will call me blessed,
　　　　for the Mighty One has done
　　　　　　great things for me—
　　　　holy is his name.
His mercy extends to those
　　　　who fear him,
　　from generation to generation.
He has performed mighty deeds
　　　　with his arm;
　　　　he has scattered those who are
　　　　　　proud in their inmost thoughts.
He has brought down rulers
　　　　from their thrones
　　but has lifted up the humble.
He has filled the hungry with
　　　　good things
　　but has sent the rich away empty.
He has helped his servant Israel,
　　remembering to be merciful

to Abraham and his
descendants forever,
even as he said to our fathers."

Mary stayed with Elizabeth for about three months and then returned home.

The Faith of Joseph
MATTHEW 1:18–24 NIV

This is how the birth of Jesus Christ came about: His mother Mary was pledged to be married to Joseph, but before they came together, she was found to be with child through the Holy Spirit. Because Joseph her husband was a righteous man and did not want to expose her to public disgrace, he had in mind to divorce her quietly.

But after he had considered this, an angel of the Lord appeared to him in a dream and said, "Joseph son of David, do not be afraid to take Mary home as your wife, because what is conceived in her is from the Holy Spirit. She will give birth to a son, and you are to give him the name, Jesus, because he will save his people from their sins."

All this took place to fulfill what the Lord has said through the prophet: "The virgin will be with child and will give birth to a son, and they will call him Immanuel"—which means, "God with us."

When Joseph woke up, he did what the angel of the Lord had commanded him and took Mary home as his wife. But he had no union with her until she gave birth to a son. And he gave him the name Jesus.

The Birth of Jesus
LUKE 2:1-20 NIV

In those days Caesar Augustus issued a decree that a census should be taken of the entire Roman world. (This was the first census that took place while Quirinius was governor of Syria.) And everyone went to his own town to register.

So Joseph also went up from the town of Nazareth in Galilee to Judea, to Bethlehem the town of David, because he belonged to the house and line of David. He went there to register with Mary, who was pledged to be married to him and was expecting a child. While they were there, the time came for the baby to be born, and she gave birth to her firstborn, a son. She wrapped him in cloths and placed him in a manger, because there was no room for them in the inn.

The Shepherds and the Angels

There were shepherds living out in the fields nearby, keeping watch over their flocks at night. An angel of the Lord appeared to them, and the glory of the Lord shone around them, and they were terrified. But the angel said to them, "Do not be afraid. I bring you good news of great joy that will be for all the people. Today in the town of David a Savior has been born to you; he is Christ the Lord. This will be a sign to you. You will find a baby wrapped in cloths and lying in a manger."

Suddenly a great company of the heavenly host appeared with the angel, praising God and saying,

> "Glory to God in the highest,
> and on earth peace to men
> on whom his favor rests."

When the angels had left them and gone into heaven, the shepherds said to one another, "Let's go to Bethlehem and see this thing that has happened, which the Lord has told us about."

So they hurried off and found Mary and Joseph, and the baby, who was lying in the manger. When they had seen him, they spread the word concerning what had been told them about this child, and all who heard ti were amazed at what the shepherds said to them. But Mary treasured up all these things and pondered them in her heart. The shepherds returned, glorifying and praising God for all the things they had heard and seen, which were just as they had been told.

Jesus Presented in the Temple

LUKE 2:21–40 NIV

On the eighth day, when it was time to circumcise him, he was named Jesus, the name the angel had given him before he had been conceived.

When the time of their purification according to the Law of Moses had been completed, Joseph and Mary took him to Jerusalem to present him to the Lord (as it is written in the Law of the Lord, "Every firstborn male is to be consecrated to the Lord"), and to offer a sacrifice in keeping with what is said in the Law of the Lord: a pair of doves or two young pigeons."

Now there was a man in Jerusalem called Simeon, who was righteous and devout. He was waiting for the consolation of Israel, and the Holy Spirit was upon him. It had been revealed to him by the Holy Spirit that he would not die before he had seen the Lord's Christ. Moved by the Spirit, he went into the temple courts. When the parents brought in the child Jesus to do for him what the custom of the Law required, Simeon took him in his arms and praised God, saying:

"Sovereign Lord, as you have
        promised
    you now dismiss your
        servant in peace.
For my eyes have seen your
        salvation,
    which you have prepared in
        the sight of all people,
a light for revelation to the
        Gentiles
and for glory to your people Israel."

The child's father and mother marveled at what was said about him. Then Simeon blessed them and said to Mary, his mother: "This child is destined to cause the falling and rising of many in Israel, and to be a sign that will be spoken against, so that the thoughts of many hearts will be revealed. And a sword will pierce your own soul too."

There was also a prophetess, Anna, the daughter of Phanuel, of the tribe of Asher. She was very old; she had lived with her husband seven years after her marriage, and then was a widow until she was eighty-four. She never left the temple but worshiped night and day, fasting and praying. Coming up to them at that very moment, she gave thanks to God and spoke about the child to all who were looking forward to the redemption of Jerusalem.

When Joseph and Mary had done everything required by the Law of the Lord, they returned to Galilee to their own town of Nazareth. And the child grew and became strong; he was filled with wisdom, and the grace of God was upon him."

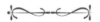

*I believe that prayer and meditation should be part of all our Christmas seasons—
that if I wait in silence, I will experience the presence of the one born in the manger,
for He lives today as surely as He lived then.*

Old-Fashioned Christmas Mix

½ cup butter
⅓ cup honey
¼ cup packed brown sugar
1 teaspoon cinnamon
½ teaspoon salt
3 cups oat cereal squares
1½ cups old-fashioned oats
1 cup small pretzels
1 cup mixed nuts

In a saucepan, combine butter, honey, brown sugar, cinnamon, and salt. Heat until butter melts and stir until sugar dissolves. In a large bowl, combine cereal, oats, pretzels, and nuts. Drizzle with butter mixture and mix well. Bake in a 9 x 13-inch pan at 275 degrees for 45 minutes. Stir every 15 minutes. Makes 6 cups.

DID YOU KNOW?

*I*magine this: Christmas trees are edible! Many parts of pines, spruces, and firs can be eaten. The needles are a good source of vitamin C. Pine nuts, or pine cones, are also a good source of nutrition.

*T*he Christmas message is that there is hope for a ruined humanity—hope of pardon, hope of peace with God, hope of glory—because at the Father's will Jesus Christ became poor, and was born in a stable so that thirty years later He might hang on a cross.

J. I. PACKER

Christmas Prayer

ROBERT LOUIS STEVENSON

Loving Father, help us remember the birth of Jesus that we may share in the song of the angels, the gladness of the shepherds, and the worship of the wise men.

Close the door of hate and open the door of love all over the world.

Let kindness come with every gift and good desires with every greeting.

Deliver us from evil by the blessing which Christ brings, and teach us to be merry with clear hearts.

May the Christmas morning make us happy to be Thy children, and the Christmas evening bring us to our beds with grateful thoughts, forgiving and forgiven, for Jesus sake. Amen.

Jesus Is the Reason for the Season

I Saw a Stable

I saw a stable, low and very bare,
A little child in a manger.
The oxen knew Him, had Him in their care,
To men He was a stranger.
The safety of the world was lying there,
And the world's danger.

MARY ELIZABETH COLERIDGE

THE NATIVITY SCENE

Saint Francis of Assisi is credited with the idea of creating a model of the nativity. He made ready a manger or crib and added hay, an ox, and a donkey. Once he had recreated the scene, it is said that he stood before the manger, bathed in tears and overwhelmed with joy.

DID YOU KNOW?

The Salvation Army has been sending Santa Claus-clad donation collectors into the streets since the 1890s.

Advent

Advent is a spiritual season of preparation before Christmas. It begins on the fourth Sunday prior to Christmas Day or the Sunday that falls closest to November 30. The season lasts through Christmas Eve.

One candle is lit each Sunday leading up to Christmas and the fifth candle is lit on Christmas Day.

Many people observe Advent as a time of gratitude to God for sending Jesus the Christ to Earth as a baby, of recognition of His presence among us today through the Holy Spirit, and of preparation and anticipation of His final coming at the end of time.

Advent Candles

Five colorful advent candles stand in the circle of an Advent wreath. Although there are variations in the colors of the candles, most often there are three purple candles, one pink, and one white. The purple represents repentance, the pink, joy, and the central white candle represents Christ. In fact, it is called the "Christ Candle." The four colored candles are often simple tapers, placed around the inside of the wreath. They are traditionally lit in the following order: purple, purple, pink, purple. The last candle, usually a large white pillar, is placed in the center and lit on Christmas Day.

The First

The First Advent Candle

The first Advent candle is called the "Candle of Hope." This purple candle symbolizes hope and expectation. It represents both the eager anticipation of a coming Messiah spoken of throughout the Old Testament and the promise that Jesus, the Messiah, will come again to earth to claim His faithful ones as described in the New Testament. Because it points to the promises that foretold Christ's birth, it is also sometimes called the "Candle of Prophecy."

dvent Candle

Suggested verses to be read at the lighting of the first candle:

Arise, shine; for your light has come! And the glory of the LORD is risen upon you. For behold, the darkness shall cover the earth, and deep darkness the people; but the LORD will arise over you, and His glory will be seen upon you.

ISAIAH 60:1-3 NKJV

You also must be ready, because the Son of Man will come at an hour when you do not expect him.

MATTHEW 24:44 NIV

41

Kings remote and legendary will pay homage,
kings rich and resplendent
will turn over their wealth.
All kings will fall down and worship.

PSALM 72:10–11 MSG

Nations have their red-letter days, their
carnivals and festivals, but once in the year,
and only once, the whole world stands still
to celebrate the advent of a life. Only Jesus
of Nazareth claims their worldwide, undying
remembrance. You cannot cut Christmas out of
the calendar, nor out of the heart of the world.

AUTHOR UNKNOWN

The Meaning of Christmas

FR. ANDREW GREELEY

*I*t might be easy to run away to a monastery, away from the commercialization, the hectic hustle, the demanding family responsibilities of Christmas-time. Then we would have a holy Christmas. But we would forget the lesson of the Incarnation, of the enfleshing of God—the lesson that we who are followers of Jesus do not run from the secular; rather we try to transform it. It is our mission to make holy the secular aspects of Christmas just as the early Christians baptized the Christmas tree. And we do this by being holy people—kind, patient, generous, loving, laughing people—no matter how maddening is the Christmas rush.

CHRISTMAS IN RUSSIA

*D*uring the communist era, many Russian Christmas traditions were suppressed, including the December 6 Feast of St. Nicholas and Babouschka, an old woman who was said to roam the countryside searching for the Christ Child and visiting the homes of children. Even Christmas trees were banned. Babouschka never really disappeared, and now that things have lightened up, she has returned openly in many homes. Russians also continue to have Christmas trees, though they have cleverly dubbed them "New Year" trees.

St. Nicholas is clearly the most popular Christmas figure in Russia. The legend is that the 11th-century Prince Vladimir traveled to Constantinople to be baptized, and returned with stories of miracles performed by St. Nicholas of Myra. After the Feast of St. Nicholas was discontinued, the saint was transformed into Grandfather Frost.

In Russia, the Christmas Eve dinner is meatless. The most important food for the occasion is a special porridge called *kutya* made of wheat berries or other grains that symbolizes hope and immortality. Honey and poppy seeds are also popular, meant to ensure happiness, success, and untroubled rest. In many homes, a priest, accompanied by boys carrying containers of holy water, sprinkle water in each room and ask that the home be blessed by God.

Christmas Tip

*I*nterested in a more ecologically-friendly Christmas? There are three easy ways to bring on "the green."

1. Buy a real tree. Most Christmas trees are grown on tree farms, specifically for Christmas tree lots. Cutting them down does not touch the preservation of the forests. In addition, artificial trees consume a significant amount of energy and petroleum-based materials during their manufacture. Be sure to recycle your tree. Rather than taking up room in a landfill, it can be ground into wood chips for area parks and gardens.

2. Recycle holiday gift wrap and give gifts that don't need to be wrapped like a homemade dinner or tickets to a game or concert.

3. Use Christmas lights with light-emitting diodes (LEDs). LEDs use the same computer-chip technology found in lighted calculators and watches. The lights are 90 percent more efficient than traditional Christmas lights.

All Year Through

Remember while December
brings the only Christmas Day,
In the year let there be Christmas
in the things you do and say;
Wouldn't life be worth the living?
Wouldn't dreams be coming true?
If we kept the Christmas spirit
all the whole year through?

AUTHOR UNKNOWN

O Holy Night

Led by the light of faith serenely beaming,
With glowing hearts by His cradle we stand.
So led by light of a star sweetly gleaming.
Here came the wise men from Orient land
The King of kings lay thus in lowly manger,
In all our trails born to be our friend!

Truly He taught us to love one another,
His law is love and His Gospel is peace.
Chains shall He break for the slave is our brother
And in His name all oppression shall cease.
Sweet hymns of joy in grateful chorus raise we;
Let all within us praise His Holy Name.

Placide Cappeau was a wine merchant and poet who lived from 1808-1877. He wrote the lyrics in response to a request for a Christmas poem by a parish priest. Adolph Adam, a French composer and music critic who lived from 1803-1856, composed the music in 1847. On December 24, 1906, this well-loved carol became the second piece of music to be broadcast on radio.

DID YOU KNOW?

*T*oday, in the Greek and Russian orthodox churches, Christmas is celebrated 13 days after the 25th, which is also referred to as the Epiphany or Three Kings Day. This is the day it is believed that the three wise men finally found Jesus in the manger.

*G*ifts of time and love are surely the basic ingredients of a truly merry Christmas.

PEG BRACKEN

Making Homemade Ornaments for the Tree

Ingredients:
1 cup cornstarch
2 cups baking soda
1½ cups cold water
String
Paint
Clear shellac

INSTRUCTIONS:

In a saucepan, stir together the cornstarch, baking soda, and water. Heat, stirring constantly until the mixture reaches a slightly moist, mashed-potato consistency. Pour onto a plate and cover with a damp cloth. When cooled, knead like dough. Roll out to a quarter-inch thickness and cut with a knife or cookie cutter. Make a hole near the top for the string. Let dry. Paint and let dry. Finish with a coat of shellac.

*T*he joy of brightening each other's lives,
Bearing each other's burdens,
Easing each other's loads,
And supplanting empty hearts and lives with
generous gifts
Becomes for us the magic of Christmas.

W. C. JONES

The Life of Our Lord for My Dear Children

CHARLES DICKENS

I am very anxious that you should know something about the history of Jesus Christ. For everyone ought to know about Him. No one ever lived who was so good, so kind, so gentle, and so sorry for all people who did wrong, or were in any way ill or miserable as He was. And as He is now in Heaven, where we hope to go, and all to meet each other after we are dead, and there be happy always together, you never can think what a good place Heaven is, without knowing who He was and what He did.

He was born a long, long time ago—nearly two thousand years ago—at a place called Bethlehem. His father and mother lived in a city called Nazareth, but they were forced by business to travel to Bethlehem. His father's name was Joseph, and His mother's name was Mary. And the town being very full of people, also brought there by business, there was no room for Joseph and Mary in the Inn or in any house; so they went into a stable to lodge, and in this stable Jesus Christ was born. There was no cradle or anything of that kind there, so Mary laid her pretty little boy in what is called a manger, which is a place the horses eat of. And there He fell asleep.

While He was asleep, some shepherds who were watching sheep in the fields saw an Angel from God, all light and beautiful, come moving over the grass towards them. At first they were afraid and fell down and hid their faces. But the angel said, "There is a child born today in the city of Bethlehem near here. He will grow up and teach men to love one another, and not to quarrel and hurt one another; and His name will be Jesus Christ." And then the angel told the shepherds to go to that stable, and look at that little child in the manger. Which they did; and they kneeled down by Him in His sleep, and said "God bless this child."

Does not the Scripture say that the Christ will come from David's family and from Bethlehem, the town where David lived?

JOHN 7:42 NIV

Glory Be to God

O holy night, O night divine!
What tender joy, what peace is thine!
For 'mid thy silence seraphs come
To herald one from heav'nly home.
But a wondrous word,
Thro' the silence heard,
It was " Glory be to God, to God on high!"

ELSIE DUNCAN YALE

There's a Song in the Air

There's a song in the air! There's a star in the sky!
There's a mother's deep prayer and a baby's low cry!
And the star rains its fire while the beautiful sing,
For the manger of Bethlehem cradles the King!

There's a tumult of joy o'er the wonderful birth,
For the virgin's sweet Boy is the Lord of the Earth.
Aye! the star rains its fire while the beautiful sing,
For the manger of Bethlehem cradles a King!

In the light of that star lie the ages impearled;
And that song from afar has swept over the world.
Every hearth is aflame, and the beautiful sing
In the homes of the nations that Jesus is King!

We rejoice in the light, and we echo the song
That comes down through the night from the
heavenly throng.
Aye! we shout to the lovely evangel they bring,
And we greet in His cradle our Savior and King!

Certainly one of the most enchanting of
Christmas carols, "There's a Song in the Air"
was written by Josiah G. Holland. Perhaps it's

the way he captured the excitement of those who witnessed the events of that holy night that gives the carol so much purity and heart. It's as if he saw what they saw with his own eyes. And maybe he did—with the eyes of his soul.

Born in Belchertown, Massachusetts, Josiah Gilbert Holland first aspired to be a doctor and graduated from medical college with honors. But he found the practice of medicine distasteful and began spending his time writing and doing editorial work. Eventually Holland helped establish *Scribner's Magazine*.

"There's a Song in the Air" first appeared in a Sunday School collection in 1874, and five years later it was included in *The Complete Poetical Writings of J.G. Holland*. The present tune was composed for these words by Karl P. Harrington approximately 25 years later. The composer was recognized as a church musician, serving in various Methodist churches as organist and choir director. He was also one of the musical editors for the Methodist Hymnal of 1905, when the present version of the carol first appeared.

Perhaps this beautiful carol is best sung while looking up at the stars and remembering the holy events of that night—the night of all nights—when the power and majesty of God came to dwell with us on earth.

The Second Advent Candle

The second Advent candle is called the "Candle of the Way." This candle is also purple and represents the truth that Christ is the only way to God. For those lost in sin, Jesus Christ is the Light sent into the world to show the way out of darkness. It is also called the "Candle of Preparation," reminding Christians to get ready to receive God.

Advent Candle

Suggested verses to be read at the lighting of the second candle:

In those days John the Baptist began preaching in the Judean wilderness. His message was, "Turn from your sins and turn to God, because the Kingdom of Heaven is near."

MATTHEW 3:1-2 NLT

Jesus told him, "I am the way, the truth, and the life. No one can come to the Father except through me."

JOHN 14:6 NLT

THE CHRISTMAS TREE

*I*t is commonly thought that Martin Luther cut down the first Christmas tree and placed candles on it to represent the starry skies of Bethlehem on the night of Christ's birth. Underneath, he placed the nativity, including Mary, Joseph, the baby Jesus, and a few animals.

I believe in the angel's message that we should not be afraid—that the Child of Bethlehem is also our Savior and Lord, the one who is able to help us overcome all our anxieties and insecurities.

Holiday Toffee Delights

    1 cup sugar
    ¼ cup water
    ½ cups chopped pecans
    1 (6 ounce) pkg. semi-sweet chocolate chips
    ½ teaspoon salt
    ½ cup butter

In a saucepan, cook sugar, water, salt, and butter to light crack stage (285 degrees). Add nuts, stir, and pour thinly onto a non-stick cookie sheet. Pour chips on top, and spread with a knife after they have melted. Sprinkle with nut pieces. Cool, break in pieces, and wrap. Yield: About one pound.

THE CHRISTMAS CAROL

*C*hristmas carols were first sung in the 4th and 5th centuries. The joyful, energetic songs commemorating the birth of Jesus Christ are thought to have been a response to the somber Christmas music that prevailed at the time. Some historical accounts say that the tradition of caroling began when the poor went from house to house singing the carols in exchange for food and drink. Others claim that carolers performed door-to-door because they were not allowed to sing carols in the churches.

DID YOU KNOW?

*F*rankincense is a sweet smelling gum resin derived from certain Boswellia trees which, at the time of Christ, grew in Arabia, India, and Ethiopia. Tradition says Balthasar, the black Magi thought to have been from Ethiopia or Saba, was the one who brought frankincense and presented it to the Christ Child. In the days of the Roman Empire, it was as valuable as many gems or precious metals.

Christmas Comes Once More

*Where charity stands watching
and faith holds wide the door,
the dark night wakes—the glory breaks,
Christmas comes once more.*

PHILLIPS BROOKS

I sometimes think we expect too much of Christmas Day. We try to crowd into it the long arrears of kindliness and humanity of the whole year. As for me, I like to take my Christmas a little at a time, all through the year. And thus I drift along into the holidays— let them overtake me unexpectedly—waking up some fine morning and suddenly saying to myself: 'Why this is Christmas Day!'

RAY STANNARD BAKER

The Sermon

PASTOR PETER MARSHALL

I thank God for Christmas. Would that it lasted all year. For on Christmas Eve, and Christmas Day, all the world is a better place, and men and women are more lovable. Love itself seeps into every heart, and miracles happen.

When Christmas doesn't make your heart swell up until it nearly bursts…and fill your eyes with tears…and make you all soft and warm inside…then you'll know that something inside of you is dead.

We hope that there will be snow for Christmas. Why? It is not really important, but it is so nice, and old-fashioned, and appropriate, we think.

Isn't it wonderful to think that nothing can really harm the joy of Christmas?

Although your Christmas tree decorations will include many new gadgets, such as lights with bubbles in them, it's the old tree decorations that mean the most, the ones you save carefully from year to year…the crooked star that goes on the top of the tree…the ornaments that you've been so careful with.

And you'll bring out the tiny manger, and

the shed, and the little figures of the Holy Family, and lovingly arrange them on the mantel or in the middle of the dining room table.

And getting the tree will be a family event, with great excitement for the children.

And there will be a closet into which you'll forbid your husband to look. And he will be moving through the house mysteriously with bundles under his coat, and you'll pretend not to notice.

There will be the fragrance of cookies baking, spices and fruitcake...and the warmth of the house shall be melodious with the lilting strains of "Silent Night, Holy Night."

And you'll listen to the wonderful Christmas music on the radio, some of the songs will be modern—good enough music perhaps—but it will be the old carols, the lovely old Christmas hymns that will mean the most.

And forests of fir trees will march right into our living rooms.... There will be bells on our doors and holly wreaths in our windows.... And we shall sweep the Noel skies for their brightest colors and festoon our homes with stars.

There will be a chubby stocking hung by the fireplace...and with finger to lip you will whisper and ask me to tiptoe, for a little tousled head is asleep and must not be awakened until after Santa has come.

And finally Christmas morning will come. Don't worry—you'll be ready for it—you'll catch the spirit all right or it will catch you, which is even better.

And then you will remember what Christmas means…the beginning of Christianity…the second Chance for the world…the hope for peace…and the only way.

The promise that the angels sang is the most wonderful music the world has ever heard. "Peace on earth and good will toward men."

I believe the most important Christmas gifts are not those under the tree—
the best gifts are the love of family and friends,
the joy of relationship with God,
and the investments we make in eternity.

Christmas Day Prayer

On this Christmas Day, we thank You, Lord:
For this place in which we dwell,
For the love that unites us.
For the peace accorded us this day,
For the hope with which we expect the morrow.
For the work, the health, the food,
For bright skies which make
our lives delightful,
For our friends in all parts of the earth.
For the Savior born to save us from our sin.
Thank You, Lord.
Amen.

Jesus Is the Reason
for the Season

Christmas Eve

The door is on the latch tonight,
The hearth fire is aglow;
I seem to hear soft passing feet—
The Christ Child in the snow.

My heart is open wide tonight,
for stranger, kith, or kin;
I would not bar a single door
where love might enter in.

AUTHOR UNKNOWN

CHRISTMAS IN ETHIOPIA

*I*n Ethiopia, the old Julian calendar is still used so Christmas, known as "Ganna" is celebrated on January 7. On January 6, Christmas Eve, people generally fast in preparation for the big day. Then early the next morning, they arise at dawn and dress in a traditional garment called a *shamma*. This is a thin, white piece of cotton with brightly colored stripes across the ends and worn like a toga. By 4:00 a.m. most everyone is assembled for the church service.

In Ethiopian villages, the churches tend to be very old and carved out of the rock. In the cities, more modern churches are built in three circles, each within the others. The choir sings from the outer circle and worshippers carry candles as they walk around the church three times in a solemn procession. Having entered the second circle, they remain standing during the service. The priests minister from the inner most circle.

Twelve days after Ganna, on January 19, Ethiopians start the three-day celebration of Timkat, which memorializes the baptism of Jesus. Children walk to church services in a procession. They wear the crowns and robes of the church youth groups they belong to. Adults wear the *shamma*. The priests wear red and white robes and carry embroidered fringed umbrellas.

Musical instruments are played during the Timkat procession. The *sistrum* is a percussion instrument with tinkling metal disks, a bit like a vertical tambourine. A *makamiya*, a long T-shaped prayer stick is used to keep the rhythm. It is also used by the priests and as a stick to lean on during the long Timkat church service.

People don't give and receive gifts during Ganna and Timkat. Sometimes children might be given a small gift of clothing by their family members. It's more a time for going to church, feasting, and playing games.

Especially in the Christmas season, the men and boys play a game called "ganna" which is similar to hockey. The sport is played with a curved stick and round wooden ball. After the Timkat church service, the men engage in *yeferas guks*. This game is played on horseback and consists of the men throwing ceremonial lances at each other.

One of the traditional Christmas foods in Ethiopia is *wat*, a thick and spicy stew containing meat, vegetables, and sometimes eggs. *Wat* is eaten on *injera*—a flat bread. Pieces of the *injera* are used as an edible spoon to scoop up the stew.

Ethiopians are proud of the traditional belief that one the Wise Men who visited Jesus was from their country.

DID YOU KNOW?

Rudolph, "the most famous reindeer of all," was the product of Robert L. May's imagination in 1939. The copywriter wrote a poem about the reindeer to help lure customers into the Montgomery Ward department store.

There's nothing sadder in this world than to awake Christmas morning and not be a child.

ERMA BOMBECK

CHRISTMAS TIP

Wondering what tip to give to whom at Christmas? Here are some ideas to go by:

1. Mail carriers that you see regularly—a gift valued at under $20. No cash.
2. Maid—if he or she works for you directly, one week's pay. If you use a service, don't tip at all.
3. Gardener—$20–$50 is fair.
4. Newspaper carrier—If your carrier delivers daily, $25-$50 works. For weekend only—$10 will be fine.
5. Teacher—a gift certificate to a bookstore or office-supply store. Keep it in the $25–$100 range.
6. Hair Stylist—$15 or more depending on how long he or she has been doing your hair.
7. Garbage Collector—$15–$20 is fine for each man on the truck. There is no need to tip if there is only a driver with an automated arm on his truck.
8. Dog Watcher or Sitter—1–2 week's pay is reasonable.

9. Baby Sitter—What you would typically pay for a night out and a gift from each of the children is also a nice touch.
10. Day-Care Provider—$25-$70 plus a small gift from your child.

*G*od grant you the light in Christmas, which is faith; the warmth of Christmas, which is love; the radiance of Christmas, which is purity; the righteousness of Christmas, which is justice; the belief in Christmas, which is truth; and all of Christmas, which is Christ.

WILDA ENGLISH

*L*et this Christmas season be a renewing of the mind and a cleansing of our lives by God's pure presence.
Let His joy come to our weary world through us.

GERALD KENNEDY

Shall I Be Silent?

The shepherds sing; and shall I silent be?
My God, no hymn for thee?
My soul's a shepherd, too; a flock it feeds
of thoughts and words and deeds:
The pasture is thy Word; the streams thy grace,
enriching all the place.

GEORGE HERBERT

*I*t is Christmas every time you let God love
others through you…
yes, it is Christmas every time you smile
at your brother and offer him your hand.

The Angel and the Shepherds

LEW WALLACE

A mile and a half, it may be two miles, southeast of Bethlehem there is a plain separated from the town by an intervening swell of the mountain. At the side farthest from the town, and close under a bluff, there was an extensive *marah*, or sheep-cote, ages old. In some long-forgotten foray the building had been unroofed and almost demolished. The enclosure attached to it remained intact, however, and that was of more importance to the shepherds who drove their charges thither than the house itself.

There were six of these men, omitting the watchman, and after a while they assembled in a group near the fire, some sitting and some lying prone. They rested and talked; and their talk was all about their flocks, a dull theme to the world, and yet a theme which was all the world to them.

While they talked, and before the first watch was over, one by one the shepherds went to sleep, each lying where he had sat. The night, like most nights of the winter season in the hill country, was clear, crisp, and sparkling with stars. There was no wind. The atmosphere seemed never so pure, the stillness was more than silence; it was a holy hush, a warning that heaven was stooping low to whisper some good thing to the listening earth.

By the gate, hugging his mantle close, the watchman walked; at times he stopped, attracted by a stir among the sleeping herd, or by a jackal's cry off on the mountainside. The midnight was slow in coming to him, but at last it came. His task was done; and now for the dreamless sleep with which labor blesses its weaned children! He moved toward the fire, but paused; a light was breaking around him, soft and white, like the moon's . He waited breathlessly. The light deepened; things before invisible came into view; he saw the whole field, and all it sheltered. A chill sharper than that of the frosty air—a chill of fear— smote him. He looked up; the stars were gone; the light was dropping as from a window in the sky; and as he looked it became a splendor; then, in terror, he cried, "Awake, awake!"

Up he sprang and the dogs, howling, ran away.

The herds rushed together, bewildered.

The men clambered to their feet, weapons in hand.

"What is it?" they asked in one voice.

"See!" cried the watchman, "the sky is on fire!"

Suddenly the light became intolerably bright, and they covered their eyes and dropped upon their knees; then as their souls shrank with fear, they fell upon their faces, blind and fainting, and would have died had not a voice said to them: "Fear not!"

And they listened.

"Fear not; for behold, I bring you good tidings of great joy, which shall be to all people. For unto you, this day, in the city of David, is born a Saviour, which is Christ the Lord! And this shall be a sign unto you, ye shall find the babe wrapped in swaddling clothes and lying in a manger."

The voice in sweetness and soothing more than human, and low and clear, penetrated all their being and filled them with assurance. They rose to their knees, and looking worshipfully up, beheld in the center of the great glory the appearance of a man, clad in a robe intensely white; above its shoulders towered the stops of wings shining and folded. A star over its forehead glowed with a steady luster, brilliant as Hesperus. Its hands were stretched toward them in blessing; its face was serene and divinely beautiful.

The herald spoke not again; his good tidings were told, and yet he stayed awhile. Then suddenly the light, of which he seemed the center, turned roseate and began to tremble.

And then up, as far as the men could see, there was a flashing of white wings, and a coming and going of radiant forms, and voices as of a whole multitude chanting in unison. "Glory to God in the highest, and on earth, peace and good will toward men!"

Then the shepherds said one to another, "Come let us take a wee ewe lamb from the fold, and yonder into Bethlehem, and see this thing which has come to pass. The priests and doctors have been a long time looking for the Christ. Now He is born, and the Lord has given us a sign by which to know Him. Let us go and worship Him."

And they followed the light until it came and stood over where the young Child lay. And they went in and found Mary and Joseph and the Child asleep in the sweet-smelling hay. And they worshiped him, leaving the wee ewe lamb without spot or blemish as their offering; and returned again to their flock on the hillside, believing anew the words of their prophets.

"Unto us a Child is born. Unto us a Son is given. And the government shall be upon His shoulder; and of the increase of His Kingdom there shall be no end. And His name shall be called, 'Wonderful, Counselor, the Mighty God, the Everlasting Father, the Prince of Peace.'"

I Heard the Bells on Christmas Day

I heard the bells on Christmas day
Their old familiar carols play,
And wild and sweet the words repeat
Of peace on earth, good will to men.

And thought how, as the day had come,
The belfries of all Christendom
Had rolled along the unbroken song
Of peace on earth, good will to men.

Till ringing, singing on its way
The world revolved from night to day,
A voice, a chime, a chant sublime
Of peace on earth, good will to men.

And in despair I bowed my head
"There is no peace on earth," I said,
"For hate is strong and mocks the song
Of peace on earth, good will to men."

Then pealed the bells more loud and deep:

"God is not dead, nor doth He sleep;
The wrong shall fail, the right prevail
With peace on earth, good will to men."

The words to this beautiful and poignant Christmas carol were written by Henry Wadsworth Longfellow on Christmas Day, 1864—a time of difficulty and heartache for the poet.

Three years earlier in 1861, just after the beginning of the Civil War, his beloved wife Frances was sealing an envelope with wax, when her dress caught fire. Though he did his best to save her, she died the next day. Now with the war in full swing, Longfellow learned that his oldest son, Charles Appleton Longfellow, had enlisted in the Union army. The poet received a letter dated March 14, 1863, which said in part, "I have tried hard to resist the temptation of going without your leave but I cannot any longer. I feel it to be my first duty to do what I can for my country and I would willingly lay down my life for it if it would be of any good." Charles was severely wounded in Virginia during the Battle of New Hope Church.

It must have been a dismal Christmas season for Longfellow. His wife gone, his son wounded, and his nation in the grip of a horrific civil war. This was the scene as the poet put his pen to paper. The poem was set to music in 1872 by John Baptiste Calkin.

Longfellow's early poetry was known for its encouraging themes. Most often his poems featured people triumphing over adversity. At his death on March 24, 1882, Walt Whitman called him a poet of all sympathetic gentleness. Certainly he was a man who chose to focus on hope, as borne out in the final stanza of this Christmas masterpiece.

:~~~~:

DID YOU KNOW?

*C*onstruction workers started the Rockefeller Center Christmas tree tradition in 1931.

Hot Holiday Fruit Punch

4 cups cranberry juice cocktail
4 cups unsweetened pineapple juice
2 cups water
½ cup firmly packed brown sugar
2 tablespoons lemon juice
2 sticks cinnamon
2 teaspoons whole cloves

Pour cranberry juice, pineapple juice and water into a large saucepan. Heat. Add brown sugar, lemon juice and cinnamon sticks and cloves. Simmer for 30 minutes. Remove cinnamon sticks and cloves. Yield: 10 cups

That Holy Star

O Father may that Holy Star
Grow every year more bright,
And send its glorious beams afar
To fill the world with light.

WILLIAM CULLEN BRYANT

The Long Walk

AUTHOR UNKNOWN

The African boy listened carefully as the teacher explained why it is that people give presents to each other on Christmas Day. "The gift is our expression of our joy over the birth of Jesus and our friendship for each other," she said.

When Christmas day came, the boy brought the teacher a sea shell of lustrous beauty. "Where did you ever find such a beautiful shell?" the teacher asked as she gently fingered the gift.

The youth told her that there was only one spot where such extraordinary shells could be found. When he named the place, a bay several miles away, the teacher was speechless.

"Why…why, it's gorgeous…wonderful, but you shouldn't have gone all that way to get a gift for me."

His eyes brightening, the boy answered, "Long walk part of gift!"

THE CHRISTMAS POINSETTIA

Native to Mexico, the Poinsettia is named after America's first ambassador to Mexico, Joel Poinsett, who brought the plants to America in 1828. In Mexican folklore, the plants were thought to be symbolic of the Star of Bethlehem because of the large, bright red leaves. The plant has been associated with Christmas since that time.

For to us a child is born, to us a son is given,
and the government will be on his shoulders.
And he will be called Wonderful Counselor,
Mighty God, Everlasting Father,
Prince of Peace. Of the increase of his
government and peace there will be no end.
He will reign on David's throne and
over his kingdom, establishing and upholding
it with justice and righteousness from
that time on and forever. The zeal of the LORD
Almighty will accomplish this.

ISAIAH 9:6–7 NIV

The Third

The Third Advent Candle

The third candle is the "Candle of Joy." This pink or rose-colored candle recalls the angels joyfully singing about the birth of Christ. It reminds us that the only lasting joy to be found on earth is through relationship with God, through the person of His Son, Jesus Christ.

Suggested verses to be read at the lighting of the third candle:

Those who have been ransomed by the LORD will return to Jerusalem, singing songs of everlasting joy. Sorrow and mourning will disappear, and they will be overcome with joy and gladness.

ISAIAH 35:10 NLT

Advent Candle

I will greatly rejoice in the LORD, my soul shall be joyful in my God; for he hath clothed me with the garments of salvation, he hath covered me with the robe of righteousness.

ISAIAH 61:10 KJV

My brothers and sisters, be full of joy in the Lord.

PHILIPPIANS 3:1 NCV

The Oxen

Christmas Eve, and the twelve of the clock.
    "Now they are all on their knees,"
An elder said as we sat in a flock
    By the embers in hearthside ease.

We pictured the meek mild creatures where
    They dwelt in their strawy pen,
Nor did occur to one of us there
    To doubt they were kneeling then.

So fair a fancy few would weave
    In these years! Yet, I feel,
If some one said on Christmas Eve,
    "Come; see the oxen kneel

In the lonely barton by yonder coomb
    Our childhood used to know,"
I should go with him in the gloom,
    Hoping it might be so.

THOMAS HARDY

*T*he perfect Christmas tree?
All Christmas trees are perfect!

CHARLES N. BARNARD

*T*he simple shepherds heard the voice of an
angel and found their Lamb; the wise men saw
the light of a star and found their Wisdom.

ARCHBISHOP FULTON J. SHEEN

*C*hristmas night, stars shine bright,
and all the angels are singing.
"The Son of God is Born!"
Little child, holy child, how I want to be near
you, this blessed Christmas night.

GARRY GAMBLE

Good News of Great Joy

DWIGHT CLOUGH

Do not be afraid.
I bring you good news of great joy.

LUKE 2:10

I remember my first Santa Claus doubts. *How could a fat man get down a skinny chimney, not just at our house, but at the houses of little boys and girls all over the world? I mean, there must be hundreds.*

Then came the fateful day when I learned the truth. Two truths, in fact. My mother was cleaning something in the living room and she said, "You know, the Easter Bunny is just make believe."

That didn't bother me. The Easter Bunny always hid the baskets behind the TV. He was expendable.

Then she added, "You know, make believe, just like Santa Claus."

I nodded like I had known all along. But inside, this revelation hurt. I wanted to believe that somewhere there was someone who cared enough about me to find out just what I wanted and to risk getting stuck in the chimney to bring it to me.

I missed Santa Claus. He had been a good friend.

I think my dad missed Santa Claus too. Now he had to take the place of the man from the North Pole. And my dad's sack of toys wasn't as big as he wanted it to be. Every December he sat us down and delivered the sad news. "I'm afraid there won't be much of a Christmas this year," he told us. "We just don't have the money."

I felt for him. I wanted to tell him it was okay.

"We don't have the money," he said and so my brother and I prepared ourselves to face the sparse holiday my father had predicted. Yet, on the morning of the 25th, we came downstairs to find our stockings stuffed and the floor beneath the tree littered with presents.

Santa slipped out of my life, and, as I grew older, a chilling realization slipped in—one that haunts me even to this day. In every city and scattered across the country, little ones with hearts full of hope hang up their stockings with care. But the man in red flies by their homes without stopping. In the morning their stockings look no different than they did the night before.

These children don't need to be told that there is no Santa Claus. They find out quite on their own.

Now I'm a dad. My little girl never heard of Santa Claus until one of the neighbors told her. And, at bedtime, she doesn't ask me to tell her about a man with toys and eight reindeer. Instead she says, "Tell me about when Jesus was born."

She knows the story well, but she asks me to tell it to her just the same.

I start with the decree from Caesar Augustus that all the world should be taxed. I tell her that Joseph and Mary had to walk a long time. And when they got to Bethlehem, no place was found for them to stay.

My daughter and I ponder that in the silence of our own thoughts. I suppose she thinks of how it would be to never find a McDonald's with a Playland and how it would be to ride on a donkey without a car seat. But I think of Joseph. There he was, pushed out of his home by a senseless decree from a Roman emperor. He comes to the town that is rightfully his own, but no one greets him. No one takes him in. Worried, he asks around for a midwife and a dry, warm, comfortable bed for Mary. "Sorry," people say. "Sorry, we can't help you." In the end, he takes shelter in a barn. And all he can offer the one he loves is a wool blanket and some straw.

I feel for him.

Then my mind goes back to my dad. I see him there at the kitchen table, sifting through a stack of bills, wondering where he will get the money to buy toys for his children. And for the little ones everywhere whose stockings are empty, I hurt. I wish I could shower gifts on them all. And I wonder, *Where is the outrage from heaven?*

My daughter tugs at my arm. "Tell me the rest of the story, Daddy."

We switch to the hills around Bethlehem. "On the night Jesus was born," I tell her, "in the hills, the sheep were sleeping—sleeping away. 'Baa. Baa.' They were dreaming sheep dreams. The shepherds were there, watching over their sheep.

"All of a sudden, an angel appeared to the shepherds! They were afraid.

"But the angel said, 'Do not be afraid.'"

My daughter always smiles when I tell her this.

"The angel said, 'I bring you good news of great joy. For tonight unto you in the city of David is born a Savior, who is Christ, the Lord. And this will be a sign unto you: You will find the baby lying in a manger.'

"And suddenly, all across the sky, the night was bright with angels. And they were singing, 'Glory to God in the highest. And on earth peace, goodwill to men.'"

My little girl's eyes get big as we look at the bedroom ceiling together. And I wonder to myself, *Can she see what my eyes cannot? Can she see the heavens filled with angels?*

What would it be like to see the heavens open? I ask myself. But, though I try, I can see no vision of angels. Instead of angels, I see a man. But he's not in a shepherd's field; he's in a hospital room. And he's not singing. He's dancing, holding his newborn daughter in his arms, filled with emotions he could never put into words. I see him there, spinning and twirling, and I realize that man is me.

"Daddy, tell me the rest of the story."

The reason for the angels' visit begins to make sense. So tonight I change the story. "What do you suppose those shepherds saw when they came to the barn where Jesus was born? Do you think they saw Joseph out in front, dancing under the stars?"

"Daddy, you are silly. They saw the baby Jesus lying in a manger."

Oh, yes. I sit there for a long time while my daughter falls asleep and dreams of angels. I sit there and think about those words from heaven: "Do not be afraid."

And, suddenly, I want to rush back through the years and talk to a little boy who grew up to be a daddy himself and say, "Have you seen the angels? Have you heard their song? Did you know that Jesus is here?"

And then I want to stop at a kitchen table

and speak to my tired and discouraged dad. "Do not be afraid. What you cannot give has been given for you."

And I want to swoop down chimneys everywhere with angels at my side and bring the good news to every little one whose heart was filled with hope. "Do not be afraid. The heavens have opened for you. The angels are here for you. Immanuel has come. Do not be afraid."

If I could, I'd bear presents to them all. Not because I think the trinkets I can give will satisfy Christmas needs. Instead, I'd bring gifts as tokens of a giving, caring God. And I'd pray that when the children finally unwrapped the paper, they'd find not a doll nor a toy truck, but rather a tiny baby, wrapped in swaddling clothes, lying in a manger.

The next morning, my wife and I are busy in the kitchen. Company is coming. Our little girl is talking to her dollies and her stuffed animals, saying this and that. We don't pay much attention, glad to have a few minutes to straighten the house and make a meal. All at once we are arrested by her words:

"Do not be afraid. For I bring you good news of great joy."

Like the angels in the darkest night,
celebrate Him.
Leaving all, go after Him like the shepherds.
Like the magi, seek Him as far
and as long as it takes.
Protect His place in your heart like Joseph,
Even if you must leave all comfort
and flee to an unfamiliar place.
Make a home in your heart for Him like Mary;
And like Mary, be prepared
to break your heart for love of Him.

*C*hristmas is the day
that holds all time together.

ALEXANDER SMITH

Though Christ a thousand
times in Bethlehem be born,
If he's not born in thee thy soul is still forlorn.

ANGELUS SILESIUS

Always Young

The earth has grown old with its burden of care
but at Christmas it always is young,
The heart of the jewel burns lustrous and fair
and its soul full of music breaks the air,
When the song of angels is sung.

PHILLIPS BROOKS

CHRISTMAS TIP

Make gift-wrapping easy with these simple tips:

1. Use the same gift wrap for every occasion by buying red, metallic silver, and white paper. Simply accentuate the paper with red, green, or metallic ribbons for your Christmas gifts.

2. Always have several shades of colored tissue paper on hand for lining gift boxes, wrapping delicate gifts, and adding a flair to gift bags. For Christmas you will need red, green, and silver.

3. Use stickers to jazz up simply decorated gifts, especially for children.

4. Create gift tags by cutting the fronts from holiday cards saved from previous years. Use double-face tape to attach them to your gifts.

5. Glue a small piece of greenery onto your wrapped gift. Fragrant pine is wonderful for Christmas gifts.

Praise the Lord, the God of Israel, because he has visited his people and redeemed them. He ahs sent us a mighty Savior from the royal line of his servant David, just as he promised through his holy prophets long ago.

LUKE 1:68–70 NLT

THE CHRISTMAS CARD

*I*n 1843, Sir Henry Cole, founder of the Victoria and Albert Museum in London, commissioned John Calcott Horsley to paint a card showing the feeding and clothing of the poor. He wanted to remind all his many friends to help the destitute at Christmas time. A center panel presented a happy family embracing one another and enjoying the festivities. "A Merry Christmas and a Happy New Year to You" was printed on the first card. One thousand cards were printed and sold for one shilling each. Thirty years later, Louis Prang, a German immigrant to the United States, published the country's first line of Christmas cards. His initial creations featured flowers and birds unrelated to the Christmas scene. By 1881, Prang was producing more than five million Christmas cards each year.

This is the message of Christmas:
We are never alone.

TAYLOR CALDWELL

Joseph's Letter Home

DR. RALPH F. WILSON

Dear Mom,

We're still in Bethlehem—Mary and I and little Jesus.

There were lots of things I couldn't talk to you about last summer. You wouldn't have believed me then, but maybe I can tell you now. I hope you can understand.

You know, Mom, I've always loved Mary. You and dad used to tease me about her when she was still a girl. She and her brothers used to play on our street. Our families got together for supper. But the hardest day of my life came scarcely a year ago when I was twenty and she only fifteen. You remember that day, don't you?

The trouble started after we were betrothed and signed the marriage agreement at our engagement. That same spring Mary had left abruptly to visit her old cousin Elizabeth in Judea. She was gone three whole months. After she got back, people started wondering out loud if she were pregnant.

It was cloudy the day when I finally confronted her with the gossip. "Mary," I asked at last, "are you going to have a baby?"

Her clear brown eyes met mine. She nodded.

I didn't know what to say. "Who?" I finally stammered.

Mom, Mary and I had never acted improperly—even after we were betrothed.

Mary looked down. "Joseph," she said. "There's no way I can explain. You couldn't understand. But I want you to know I've never cared for anyone but you." She got up, gently took my hands in hers, kissed each of them as if it were the last time she would ever do that again, and then turned toward home. She must have been dying inside. I know I was.

The rest of the day I stumbled through my chores. It's a wonder I didn't hurt myself in the woodshop. At first I was angry and pounded out my frustrations on the doorframe I was making. My thoughts whirled so fast I could hardly keep my mind on my work. At last I decided just to end the marriage contract with a quiet divorce. I loved her too much to make a public scene.

I couldn't talk to you. Or anyone, for that matter. I went to bed early and tried to sleep. Her words came to me over and over. "I've never cared for anyone but you—I've never cared for anyone but you—" How I wished I could believe her!

I don't know when I finally fell asleep. Mom, I had a dream from God. An angel of the

Lord came to me. His words pulsated through my mind so intensely I can remember them as if it were yesterday.

"Joseph, son of David," he thundered, "do not fear to take Mary home as your wife, because what is conceived in her is from the Holy Spirit."

I couldn't believe my ears, Mom. This was the answer! The angel continued, "She will give birth to a son, and you are to give him the name Jesus, because he will save his people from their sins."

The angel gripped my shoulders with his huge hands. For a long moment his gaze pierced deep within me. Just as he turned to go, I think I saw a smile on his shining face.

I sat bolt upright in bed. No sleep after that! I tossed about for a while, going over the words in my mind. Then I got up and dressed quietly so I wouldn't wake you.

I must have walked for miles beneath the moonless sky. Stars pricked the blackness like a thousand tiny pinpoints. A warm breeze blew on my face.

I sang to the Lord, Mom. Yes, me, singing, if you can imagine that. I couldn't contain my joy. I told Him that I would take Mary and care for her. I told Him I would watch over her—and the child—no matter what anyone said.

I got back just as the sun kissed the hilltops. I don't know if you still recall that morning, Mom. I can see it in my mind's eye as if it were yesterday. You were feeding the chickens, surprised to see me out. Remember?

"Sit down," I said to you. "I've got to tell you something." I took your arm and helped you find a seat on the big rock out back. "Mom," I said, "I'm going to bring Mary home as my wife. Can you help make a place for her things?"

You were silent a long time. "You do know what they're saying, don't you, son?" you said at last, your eyes glistening.

"Yes, Mom, I know."

Your voice started to rise. "If your father were still alive, he'd have some words, I'll tell you. Going about like that before you are married. Disgracing the family and all. You...you and Mary ought to be ashamed of yourselves!"

You'd never have believed me if I'd tried to explain, so I didn't. Unless the angel had spoken to you, you'd have laughed me to scorn.

"Mom, this is the right thing to do," I said.

And then I started talking to you as if I were the head of the house. "When she comes I don't want one word to her about it," I sputtered. "She's your daughter-in-law, you'll respect her. She'll need your help if she's to bear the neighbors' wagging tongues!"

I'm sorry, Mom. You didn't deserve that. You started to get up in a huff.

"Mom," I murmured, "I need you." You took my hand and got to your feet, but the fire was gone from your eyes.

"You can count on me, Joseph," you told me with a long hug. And you meant it. I never heard another word. No bride could hope for a better mother-in-law than you those next few months.

Mom, after I left you I went up the road to Mary's house and knocked. Her mother glared at me as she opened the door. Loudly, harshly she called into the house, "It's Joseph!" almost spitting out my name as she said it.

My little Mary came out cringing, as if she expected me to give her the back of my hand, I suppose. Her eyes were red and puffy. I can just imagine what her parents had said.

We walked a few steps from the house. She looked so young and afraid. "Pack your things, Mary," I told her gently. "I'm taking you home to be my wife."

"Joseph!" She hugged me as tight as she could. Mom, I didn't realize she was so strong.

I told her what I'd been planning. "We'll go

to Rabbi Ben-Ezer's house this week and have him perform the ceremony."

I know it was awfully sudden, Mom, but I figured the sooner we got married the better it would be for her, and me, and the baby.

"Mary, even if our friends don't come, at least you and I can pledge our love before God." I paused. "I think my Mom will be there. And maybe your friend Rebecca would come if her dad will let her. How about your parents?"

I could feel Mary's tiny frame shuddering as she sobbed quietly.

"Mary," I said. I could feel myself speaking more boldly. "No matter what anyone says about you, I'm proud you're going to be my wife. I'm going to take good care of you. I've promised God that."

She looked up.

I lowered my voice. "I had a dream last night, Mary. I saw an angel. I know."

The anguish that had gripped her face vanished. She was radiant as we turned away from the house and began to walk up the hill together.

Just then her mother ran out into the yard. "Wait," she called. She must have been listening from behind the door. Tears were streaming down her cheeks.

"I'll get your father," she called, almost giddy with emotion. "We," she cried as she gathered up her skirts. "We," she shouted as she began to run to find her husband. "We…are going to have a wedding!"

That's how it was, Mom. Thanks for being there for us. I'll write again soon.

Love, Joseph[1]

It is the personal thoughtfulness, the warm human awareness, the reaching out of the self to one's fellow man that makes giving worthy of the Christmas spirit.

ISABEL CURRIER

Animal Crackers are not really crackers, but cookies imported to the United States from England in the late 1800s. Barnum's circus-like boxes were designed with a string handle so that they could be hung on a Christmas tree.

This Good News was promised long go by God through his prophets in the holy Scriptures. It is the Good News about his Son, Jesus, who came as a man, born into King David's royal family line.

ROMANS 1:2–3 NLT

CHRISTMAS IN EGYPT

*T*hough it might be difficult to believe, Christmas is one of the most popular festivals in Egypt. The birth of Christ is celebrated by both Christians and Muslims. Egyptians feel they have a special part in the celebration of the holy event because they gave refuge to the Holy Family when they fled to Egypt as the angel directed Joseph.

Christmas in Egypt is celebrated on January 7 rather than December 25. There is a great deal of diversity in how the holiday is celebrated. But most common traditions include attending church in bright-colored clothing. During the Christmas season, the church is decorated with lamps and candles. The service lasts until midnight, followed by the ringing of the church bells.

After the service, congregants gather to receive the special bread called *"qurban,"* which means sacrifice. This is a variation on the Christian sacrament of communion. The bread is served with wine, which symbolizes the body and blood of Jesus. The bread is marked by a cross in the middle and 12 dots that represent the 12 apostles. A special Christmas meal, known as *"fata"* is served in their homes, which consists of bread, rice, garlic, and boiled meat. The next morning, celebrants visit friends and neighbors to exchange *"kaik"* (a type of shortbread) which is eaten with a drink called *"shortbat."*

Our Quest

It is in loving—not in being loved
The heart is blest;
It is in giving—not in seeking gifts
We find our quest.

Whatever be your longing and your need—
That you should give;
So shall your soul be fed,
And you indeed shall truly live.

AUTHOR UNKNOWN

Christmas Morning Sausage-Cheese Bake

½ pound pork sausage
9 eggs, beaten
3 cups milk
½ teaspoon dry mustard
1 teaspoon salt
3 slices bread, cut into ½-inch cubes
1½ cups (6 ounces) shredded cheddar
   cheese
Green pepper rings
Fresh parsley springs
Cherry tomatoes

Cook sausage over medium heat until done, stirring to crumble. Drain well on paper towels; set aside. Combine the sausage and all remaining ingredients except garnishes, mixing well. Pour into a well-greased 13 x 9 x 2-inch baking pan. Cover and refrigerate overnight. Bake at 350 degrees for 1 hour. Garnish with a cluster of green pepper rings, parsley, and cherry tomatoes. Yield: 8-10 servings

The Fourth

The Fourth Advent Candle

The fourth candle, the "Candle of Love." This purple candle reminds us that God loves us enough to send His only Son to Earth. It is also sometimes called the "Candle of Peace" because it reminds us that Jesus comes to bring Peace to both the world and people's hearts. Without Christ there is no peace in this world.

Advent Candle

Suggested verses to be read at the lighting of the fourth candle:

A child is born to us, a son is given to us. And the government will rest on his shoulders. These will be his royal titles: Wonderful Counselor, Mighty God, Everlasting Father, Prince of Peace. His ever-expanding, peaceful government will never end.

Isaiah 9:6–7 nlt

Because of God's tender mercy, the light from heaven is about to break upon us, to give light to those who sit in darkness and in the shadow of death, and to guide us to the path of peace.

Luke 1:78–79 nlt

*C*hristmas! The very word brings joy to our hearts. No matter how we may dread the rush, the long Christmas lists for gifts and cards to be bought and given—when Christmas Day comes there is still the same warm feeling we had as children, the same warmth that enfolds our hearts and our homes.

JOAN WINMILL BROWN

DID YOU KNOW?

Candy canes began as straight white sticks of sugar candy used to decorate Christmas trees. A choirmaster at Cologne Cathedral was said to have bent the ends to depict a shepherd's crook. He passed the candy canes out to the children to keep them quiet during Christmas service. Red stripes were not added to the candy until the 20th century.

Go Tell It on the Mountain

While shepherds kept their watching
O'er silent flocks by night,
Behold throughout the heavens,
There shone a holy light.

The shepherds feared and trembled
When lo! Above the earth
Rang out the angel chorus
That hailed our Savior's birth.

Down in a lowly manger
Our humble Christ was born,
And God sent us salvation
That blessed Christmas morn.

Chorus:
Go tell it on the mountain,
Over the hills and everywhere;
Go tell it on the mountain
That Jesus Christ is born!

Created in the 19th century, this spiritual is considered by many to be the finest ever written. It is thought to be anonymous, but some say it could be the creation of Frederick J. Work, an African-American from Tennessee.

Behold the virgin shall be with child,
and shall bear a Son,
and they shall call His name Immanuel,
which translated means,
"God with us."

MATTHEW 1:23 NASB

I believe that Christmas is a time for
remembering Christ and the incarnation of
God's love in human flesh.
That truth shines brighter than
any Christmas light or ornament.

CHRISTMAS TIP

Store ornaments in a box filled with shredded newspaper. This will protect the ornaments without having to wrap them separately. Cover the box of ornaments in brightly colored Christmas wrap so it can be found easily in the attic, on shelves, or in closets.

DID YOU KNOW?

Turkey was a popular choice for Christmas dinner in Victorian England. Many of the birds were raised in Norfolk, and *walked* to market in London. To protect their feet from the frozen mud on the roads, the turkeys wore little boots made of sacking or leather. Geese were not so lucky. Their feet were simply painted with tar.

Some Say

Some say that ever 'gainst that season comes
Wherein our Savior's birth is celebrated,
The bird of dawning singeth all night long;
And then, they say, no spirit dare stir abroad;
The nights are wholesome; then no planets strike,
No fairy takes, nor witch hath power to charm,
So hallow'd and so gracious is the time.

WILLIAM SHAKESPEARE

Chocolate Angel Pie

2 egg whites
1/8 teaspoon salt
1/8 teaspoon cream of tartar
½ cup sugar
½ teaspoon vanilla extract
½ cup finely chopped walnuts or pecans
1 (4-ounce) package sweet baking chocolate
3 tablespoons water
1 teaspoon vanilla extract
1 cup whipping cream, whipped

Beat egg whites (at room temperature), salt and cream of tartar until foamy. Gradually add sugar, 2 tablespoons at a time, beating until stiff peaks form. Fold in ½ teaspoon vanilla and walnuts or pecans. Spoon the meringue into a lightly greased 8-inch pie plate. Use a spoon to shape meringue into a pie shell, swirling sides ½ inch above the edge of the pie plate. Bake at 300 degrees for 50-55 minutes. Cool.

Combine chocolate and water in a small saucepan; cook over low heat, stirring constantly, until melted and smooth. Stir in 1 teaspoon vanilla; cool. Fold in whipped cream; spoon into meringue shell. Refrigerate at least 2 hours. Yield: one 8-inch pie.

DID YOU KNOW?

Homemade decorations were the norm at early Christmas celebrations—paper flowers, apples, biscuits, sweets of all kinds. The earliest store-bought decorations came from Nuremburg, Germany. The city of Lauscha, Germany is famous for the first glass ornaments. In the late 1800s, F. W. Woolworth bought a few glass ornaments from Lauscha. They sold out quickly, so the next year they bought more. When the popular glass ornaments became unavailable during World War I, American manufacturers decided to make their own, an industry still flourishing today.

Wonder

Shall I tell you what I saw?
Camels tethered at the door.
Costly gifts upon the floor
Kings a-kneeling in the straw,
Lost in wonder, pale with awe,
While a Child, smile!

DAWN FINLAY

Love Came Down at Christmas

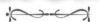

Love came down at Christmas,
Love all lovely, Love Divine;
Love was born at Christmas,
Star and Angels gave the sign.

Worship we the Godhead,
Love Incarnate, Love Divine;
Worship we our Jesus:
But wherewith for sacred sign?

Love shall be our token,
Love shall be yours and love be mine,
Love to God and all men,
Love for plea and gift and sign.

This lovely Christmas poem written by Christina Georgina Rossetti was first published without a title in *Time Flies: A Reading Diary* in 1885. In 1893, it was included in a collection simply entitled *Christmastide*.

Rossetti began writing down and dating her poems in 1842, shortly after her family suffered severe financial difficulties due to a decline in her father's health. The poetess was just twelve years old. At the age of fourteen, she suffered a nervous breakdown followed by bouts of illness. During that time of emotional need, Christina became interested in an Anglo-Catholic movement and devotion to God became a big part of her life and writing. She began to produce sonnets, hymns, and ballads, drawing heavily from the Bible, folk tales, and the lives of the saints. Christina continued to write—primarily devotional writing and poetry for children—until she died of breast cancer a few days after Christmas in 1894.

The poem has been set to music by many composers through the years. It is sung to the traditional Irish melody "Garton." In 2007, a band called Jars of Clay gave the song a modern treatment and included it in their album, *Christmas Songs*.

The Fifth

The Fifth Advent Candle

The fifth Advent candle is the "Christ Candle." It is a large white pillar candle that goes in the middle of the Advent wreath. It symbolizes Jesus Christ Himself, reminding us that He was willing to give up His throne in heaven and become one of us so that we might be reconciled to God our Father. It puts us in remembrance that He is now seated in heaven at the right hand of His Father.

Advent Candle

Suggested verses to be read at the lighting of the Christ candle:

Since we have been made right in God's sight by faith, we have peace with God because of what Jesus Christ our Lord has done for us.

ROMANS 5:1 NLT

God, who said, "Let there be light in the darkness," has made us understand that the light is the brightness of the glory of God that is seen in the face of Jesus Christ.

2 CORINTHIANS 4:6 NLT

DID YOU KNOW?

After "A Christmas Carol," Charles Dickens wrote several other Christmas stories, one each year, but none was as successful as the original.

*I*t is Christmas in the heart
that puts Christmas in the air.

W. T. ELLIS

Cinnamon-Sugared Pecans

2 cups pecan halves
1 cup sugar
1 tablespoon butter
½ cup milk
½ teaspoon salt
1 tablespoon cinnamon

Combine sugar, butter, milk, salt and cinnamon in a saucepan. Cook to the soft-ball stage or until a drop of the mixture forms a soft ball when dropped into cold water. Add pecans and cook until the mixture granulates (about five minutes). Spoon the mixture onto a butter cookie sheet. When it is hardened, break into pieces.

Jesus was born in the town of Bethlehem in Judea, during the reign of King Herod. About that time some wise men from eastern lands arrived in Jerusalem, asking "Where is the newborn king of the Jews? We have seen his star as it arose," and we have come to worship him." Herod was deeply disturbed by their question, as was all of Jerusalem. He called a meeting of the leading priests and teachers of religious law. "Where did the prophets say the Messiah would be born?" he asked them. "In Bethlehem," they said, "for this is what the prophet wrote:

O Bethlehem of Judah,
you are not just a lowly village of Judah,
for a ruler will come from you
who will be the shepherd for my people Israel.

Then Herod sent a private message to the wise men, asking them to come see him. At this meeting, he learned the exact time when they first saw the star. Then he told them, "Go to Bethlehem and search carefully for the child. And when you find him, come back and tell

me so that I can go and worship him, too!"
After this interview the wise men went their
way. Once again the star appeared to them,
guiding them to Bethlehem. It went ahead of
them and stopped over the place where the child
was. When they saw the star, they were filled
with joy! They entered the house where the
child and his mother, Mary, were, and they fell
down before him and worshiped him. Then they
opened their treasure chests and gave him gifts
of gold, frankincense, and myrrh. But when it
was time to leave, they went home another way,
because God had warned them in a dream not
to return to Herod.

MATTHEW 2:1–12 NLT

How silently,
How silently
the wonderous gift is given.
So God imparts to human hearts
The wonders of His heaven.

PHILLIPS BROOKS

Christmas gift suggestions:
To your enemy, forgiveness.
To an opponent, tolerance.
To a friend, your heart.
To a customer, service.
To all, charity.
To every child, a good example.
To yourself, respect.

The work of Christmas is to:
Find the lost,
Heal those broken in spirit,
Feed the hungry,
Release the oppressed,
Rebuild the nations,
Bring peace among all peoples,
Make a little music with the heart.

HOWARD THURMAN

Christmas Eve was a night of song that wrapped itself about you like a shawl. But it warmed more than your body. It warmed your heart . . . filled it, too, with a melody that would last forever.

BESS STREETER ALDRICH

A Night Wrapped in Song

LYDIA E. HARRIS

The chilly wind blew as I huddled with other carolers outside our country church. I drew in the cold, crisp night air, shivering with excitement. After years of waiting, my turn had come. I was finally old enough to carol all night with the church choir. With church folk scattered throughout the rural area around Blaine, Washington, it would take most of the night to carol at each member's doorstep. Bundled in my green woolen scarf and new gloves, I couldn't wait to begin.

I remembered past Christmas Eves when I had watched my seven older brothers and sisters leave the warmth of our family gathering at 11 p.m. to carol. How I had longed to go with them. At bedtime, I would beg my mother, "Please, wake me when the carolers come." She always tried, but sometimes she couldn't rouse me.

As I grew older, my mother found it easier to awaken me in the middle of the night. Sleepy-eyed and pajama-clad, I would peek out the dormer window of our large green-and-white farmhouse. I would listen dreamily to the carolers with my nose pressed against the frosty window. They sounded like angels, singing, "Joy to the World" and "Silent Night." I returned their cheerful shouts of "Merry Christmas!" and nestled back in bed, wishing I could join the fun.

Now, after years of yearning and waiting, my turn had come at last. The wind nipped my rosy cheeks. *A few snowflakes would make it perfect*, I thought. The choir director's voice interrupted my dreaming.

"Let's get organized," he said. "How many of you can take your cars?" I looked around at the young men offering to drive. I hoped to sit in the front seat between a couple of them. But other teenage girls experienced at flirting won those seats. I piled into the backseat with friends, just excited to be going along.

We laughed and chatted as we drove

through the countryside, stopping to sing for church members. By starlight and flashlight, we *crunch, crunch, crunched* our way over the frozen ground to the front doors of farmers' homes. Most folks expected us and flung their doors wide open, inviting us in for a snack, even at two or three a.m. Sipping hot chocolate by the crackling fires warmed us inside and out. Their generous hospitality forced the choir director to limit the number of families allowed to feed us. Otherwise, we'd get sick from feasting in each home. Even so, we waddled to the cars stuffed like fat Christmas geese.

We continued to the next homes, refueled with Sloppy Joes, hot dogs, and fudge. As the night wore on, our throats wore out from singing in the winter air. We sounded more like croaking frogs than the angelic choir I remembered hearing as a child.

Arriving home at five a.m., I snuggled beneath my thick handmade quilt. I tried to snatch a few hours of sleep before the Christmas morning church service where the choir would sing again. But it seemed hard to fall asleep with the excitement so fresh in my mind.

The night had been better than I imagined. No, I didn't hear angelic hosts sing, "Glory to God in the highest" to country shepherds, but I sang of His birth to country church members. I didn't see one, bright star in the sky, but I sang by starlight about that "star of wonder, star of night." I didn't bow at a manger to touch a newborn infant, but God touched me as I worshipped the newborn King when I sang, "O come, let us adore Him."

More than forty years later, all-night caroling on Christmas Eve remains a treasured memory. I savor those magical nights wrapped in song that warmed me like my new woolen scarf.

A few years ago, I returned to the Mennonite church of my childhood and asked the pianist, "Does the choir still carol all night on Christmas Eve?"

Her face broke into a wide grin. "We sure do!"

This Christmas Eve in northwestern Washington, carolers will again awaken sleepy-eyed children and serenade waiting families. They'll stuff themselves with homemade treats throughout the frosty night. And little ones will long to join the caroling choir and sing praises to the Christ Child under starlit skies.

It cheers my heart to know the caroling tradition lives beyond my dreams, creating treasured memories for another generation of youthful carolers.

INDEX

Essays

Miscellaneous

Poems

Stories

End Notes

   A Night Wrapped in Song by Lydia Harris. Used by permission of the author.

   Good News of Great Joy by Dwight Clough. Used by permission of the author.

   Joseph's Letter Home by Dr. Ralph Wilson. Used by permission of the author.